THE
SET
DOOR

DR. ADENIKE GBENLE

DEDICATION

To my late younger brother, Olutope Oladipupo Majaro. Even though you were younger, you taught me wisdom and how to love God. You were a visionary, songwriter, preacher, praise and worship leader and mentor. You founded Beautiful Feet (a ministry that mentored many young men and women) and authored *The Vision is Not Impossible.* You lived life very fast and left too soon, but your impact in my life and in the lives of others lives on! We love you and miss you.

ACKNOWLEDGMENTS

I can boldly and confidently say my life is a product of the grace of God. Therefore, I must appreciate and acknowledge the vessels that God has continued to use to keep me basking in His grace.

I appreciate my spiritual parents, Bishop David and Pastor (Mrs.) Faith Oyedepo of the Living Faith Church Worldwide, for their tremendous spiritual input in my life. I have also been blessed by the ministries of Bishop David and Pastor (Mrs.) Mary Abioye, and Bishop Thomas and Pastor (Mrs.) Elizabeth Aremu.

Pastor Chibuike Nwafor left indelible marks in my life, as a worthy mentor. He recognized and helped me see what God has placed in me. I also celebrate Pastor Isaac Oyedepo, who has been a dynamic spiritual leader and whose teachings inspired me to write this book.

My life has been filled with love from my family. God deliberately located and situated my sweet husband and partner, Ademola, who has been my pillar of support and encouragement for the past twenty years. I could not have asked God for a better partner, whose love and understanding have allowed me to tread divine paths and find fulfillment in life. I also want to recognize Ayomide, Iyanu, and Tobi, my three wonderful children, who have been remarkably supportive by pushing and cheering their mommy to complete this book project.

I also thank God for my sweet mother, who made sacrifices, raising us with everything that she had. You are indeed a mother that anyone could ever ask for. My loving sister, Tosin, for your love and support all through the years is immeasurable.

CONTENTS

INTRODUCTION

Growing up in a suburban part of Lagos, Nigeria, was an experience I will never forget. We shuttled between two houses on streets right next to each other. The one street was named after my family, "Majaro.". This street led to the back gate of the University of Lagos, a renowned university in the country. The family house was where everyone lived. We stayed with Grandma after school, until Mom came back in the evening to take us to our second home on Johnson Street, which was the rented single room where my parents birthed and raised us, until my teenage years. Every morning I would walk to and from school. My grandmother was a trader who sold fish, and fish was pretty much what we ate every day for lunch. Any day that we had to eat chicken was a major day of joy and celebration.

One would think that the house on Majaro Street would be the best looking, since the street derived its name from it; but it was the poorest looking house on the whole street. It was, however, full of love. The house also had many orchards, with all manner of fruits grown. The mango season was particularly special, as my uncles would climb up the trees to pluck the mangos, heap them into big basins, and put them in front of the house, so every passerby got a fruit. At night we would all gather to play games. It was fun!

The Johnson Street house was similar to that on Majaro, having up to eight tenants living in a single room; it was not an apartment. The bathroom and the kitchen were shared by all, and each person had a corner to cook. Thinking back about it, it was really an unbelievable sight; but God kept us. There was always war in the building - either among the tenants, or between the landlady and her children. Even more disturbing is that each of the tenants lost, at least, a child; except my mother. My mom was spiritual, and we regularly went to church. I believe my mom's faith in God kept us alive.

My mother was a single mom and a medical laboratory scientist who had studied histopathology and parasitology. She was able to get a job at the Lagos University Teaching Hospital (LUTH) as a medical lab scientist. This was a lifesaver for us. My mom used her decent salary to send us to private school. My father was alive but absent in our lives. I watched my mother struggle every day trying to make ends meet.

The beginning of our breakthrough was when Mom was able to save enough money to buy us a home far away from the "Johnson house of horror". Even though the windows of the new house were not completely done yet, my mom was desperate to get us out of harm's way after another tenant lost her child and the question was "who is next?"

It was a race of desperation to move out, and God made it possible. With all the struggles, God kept us all the way, even though we did not quite know Him.

It was not until 1996 that I got to know Christ Jesus as my Lord and personal Savior, after surrendering my life to Him. This decision of salvation was my set door into a new world of victorious living with Jesus. He brought me and my family out of the miry clay and set our feet upon the Rock of Ages that never fails.

Salvation really is the first step out of a world of chaos and randomness. There is indeed no other foundation that a man can lay other than that that is in Christ Jesus. This foundation of salvation is the opener to your set door of greatness in life.

CHAPTER ONE

YOUR NAMED DOOR

"I know thy works: behold, I have set before thee an open door, and no man can shut it: for thou hast a little strength, and hast kept my word, and hast not denied my name."
(Revelation 3:8).

There is a door with your name on it. A door that God has created for you only. Even though there are many doors in the journey of life, there is a set door prepared by God for you alone – an incomparable door, with only your name on it.

Many are struggling and are frustrated, trying to unlock doors that they have no access keys to. As a result, they experience stagnation and abandonment of purpose. You cannot have access through a door that you do not have the key to.

Crying and weeping, praying and fasting, many are hopelessly standing at doors that do not belong to them. There is a set door for your ministry, career, family, and business. There is a door with your name on it. Standing at the wrong door is suicidal because you could be mistaken for a thief and meet an untimely death. That shall not be your portion, in Jesus' name.

If it is not your door, then you cannot have the key to access. God will not let you through another person's door. Any attempt to break into someone else's home will typically lead to an arrest for burglary, which brings untold pain. So, stop wishing and hoping the wrong door opens for you.

You can only have access to the set door ordained by your heavenly Father who created you and designed it. Doors have variations in their make, style, beauty. There are doors of steel, wood, fiber glass, aluminum - you name it. However, regardless of how gigantic or beautiful a door is, *the key to enter is the access code.* Access comes through the key. No key, no entry!

Who Sets the Door?

I have good news for you today: God alone sets the door!! Here is Revelation 3:8 again:

"... behold, I have set before thee an open door, and no man can shut it..."

Hallelujah!

God is the "door setter." No man or connection can lead you, let alone open the set door Christ has for you. Only Jesus can open it, and only He can shut it.

"I am the door: by me if any man enter in, he shall be saved, and shall go in and out, and find pasture" (John 10: 9).

I pray that, by the power of the Holy Ghost, you will supernaturally access every preordained door set for you by God, through the keys you will receive as you read this book. This is your time, in Jesus' name!

Reflections Questions

What doors are you trying to unlock but do not have access to?

What does the set door that God has created only for you look like for your family, ministry, career and business?

How will you begin to seek God for the set door that He has set specifically for you?

Chapter Two

Prequalifiers for Your Set Door: Salvation

*"I know thy works: behold, **I have set** before thee an open door, and no man can shut it: for thou hast a little strength, and hast kept my word, and hast not denied my name."* (Revelation 3:8).

The above verse highlights the three prequalifying elements for accessing your set door: salvation, your works, and faith.

Salvation is the number one prequalifier to your set door of purpose, joy, and breakthrough in the Kingdom. In Revelation 3:8, Jesus – the author and the finisher of our faith – says, *"I have set before thee an open door"*. Jesus has the key that opens the door of unending breakthrough, but we must first know Him as the door, through salvation. In John 10:9, Jesus states, *"I am the door: by me if any man enter in, he shall be saved, and shall go in and out, and find pasture."* If you do not know Him who is the "door", then you cannot have access to the pasture behind the door. You don't gain access to your rental property without first collecting the key from your landlord. Jesus is the landlord of your set door of breakthroughs and abundance; but the question is, are you in a relationship with Him? Do you know Jesus as your "door setter" or "door opener"? Jesus is the only authentic key to your set door.

"And to the angel of the church in Philadelphia write; These things saith he that is holy, he that is true, he that hath the key of David, he that openeth, and no man shutteth; and shutteth, and no man openeth" (Revelation 3:7).

Let me pause here to remind you that there are doors, and there are ***doors***. There are doors made of clay, wood, brass, iron, or gold. People behind these doors are drinking, marrying, and thinking they have a life. They smile on the outside while crying on the inside. They pretend all day, but at night they cry in their beds because they have no joy or peace.

People behind these doors may have a fleet of cars and businesses; they may have even built luxury houses. But they mostly live in a state of sickness and disease, with failed marriages and prodigal children. They lack both joy and peace.

There is a front door and a back door; you have the option to choose either. But remember that the only guaranteed door is the true door. Today, you must decide.

"I call heaven and earth to record this day against you, that I have set before you life and death, blessing and cursing: therefore choose life, that both thou and thy seed may live" (Deuteronomy 30:19).

"Jesus saith unto him, I am the way, the truth, and the life: no man cometh unto the Father, but by me" (John 14:6).

The Bible says in Proverbs 10:22 that *"the blessing of the Lord, it maketh rich, and he addeth no sorrow with it."* The SET DOOR I talk about in this book is the door of unending joy and peace in the Holy Ghost. The set door has no sickness behind it. The set door is the one that makes you the light of the world and enables you to become a city set on the hill. Enter that door, and you become the envy of your world. That door makes you a blessing to your generation and the world. That door sets you at the feet of Jesus and not away from Him. This is the set door.

Again, there is a set door with your name on it, and God will grant you access to it, in Jesus' name – but that is only if you know Him, if you surrender your life to Him, and if you become born again. I have a question for you today — Where do you stand?

Today will mark the end of your struggle, if you will quit (going through) the back door and come through the front door, the straight door that is Jesus. You do this by surrendering your life afresh to Him. He is the Lifter of your head, the Bright and Morning Star. He is Jesus Christ, the Lord!

Today is the day of your salvation, giving you access to your set door!! Choose life, and you shall live!

Prayer

Lord Jesus, I surrender, and I rededicate my life to you today.

19

Forgive me my sins and wash me in your precious blood. Today, receive me into your Kingdom. I believe that you died for me, and you rose on the third day that I might have life abundantly in you. Today, I am born again, in Jesus' name.

Congratulations! It is a new day for you and your set door is waiting to be accessed by you.

Reflection Questions

Since salvation is the main prequalifier for your set door, what is your testimony?

What are the areas that the Lord is asking you to surrender to Him so that you can open your set door?

CHAPTER THREE

PREQUALIFIERS FOR YOUR SET DOOR: YOUR WORKS

*"I know thy works: behold, I have set before thee an open
door, and no man can shut it: for thou hast a little strength,
and hast kept my word, and hast not denied my name"
(Revelation 3:8).*

The second prequalifier for your set door is in the
phrase, *"I know thy works."* James 2:14-26 elaborates
on this:

*"What doth it profit, my brethren, though a man say he hath
faith, and have not works? can faith save him? If a brother
or sister be naked, and destitute of daily food, And one of
you say unto them, Depart in peace, be ye warmed and filled;
notwithstanding ye give them not those things which are needful
to the body; what doth it profit? Even so faith, if it hath not
works, is dead, being alone. Yea, a man may say, Thou hast
faith, and I have works:* **shew me thy faith without thy
works, and I will shew thee my faith by my works.**
*Thou believest that there is one God; thou doest well: the devils
also believe, and tremble. But wilt thou know, O vain man, that*

faith without works is dead? Was not Abraham our father justified by works, when he had offered Isaac his son upon the altar? Seest thou how faith wrought with his works, and by works was faith made perfect? And the scripture was fulfilled which saith, Abraham believed God, and it was imputed unto him for righteousness: and he was called the Friend of God. Ye see then how that by works a man is justified, and not by faith only. Likewise also was not Rahab the harlot justified by works, when she had received the messengers, and had sent them out another way? For as the body without the spirit is dead, so faith without works is dead also."

Does Jesus know your works? I know you have faith, and you are a Christian, but do you have works to show for it? Where are your works of service to God, to your neighbors, to the widows, and to the homeless on the street? Where are your works of praying Kingdom-advancing prayers? Where are your works of dedication and commitment to the work of God in your service group and beyond? Where are your works of winning souls and feeding the hungry?

Show me your faith, and I will show you my works. Your faith is meaningless without your works! Jesus is saying to you this day, show me your works, and I will open your set door!

Hallelujah!

The Abrahamic Set Door

"Was not Abraham our father justified by works, when he had offered Isaac his son upon the altar?" (James 2:21)

In Genesis 12, God made a promise to bless Abraham - who was at the time known as Abram - and his seed, which would come through his wife Sarah (Sarai). The life of Abraham represents a door that God had for him and his seed through Sarah. The Abrahamic set door is one of faith justified by works. Although Abraham fathered Ishmael through Sarah's handmaid, Hagar, God intended His covenant to be established with the son Abraham and Sarah would have – Isaac. Therefore, Abraham's willingness to offer up his promised son, Isaac, as a sacrifice to obey God was a great demonstration of faith.

"And he said, Take now thy son, thine only son Isaac, whom thou lovest, and get thee into the land of Moriah; and offer him there for a burnt offering upon one of the mountains which I will tell thee of" (Genesis 22:2).

Abraham went all the way, prepared with all that was needed to sacrifice his son, making sure he left nothing behind - including the knife that he would need to make the sacrifice. Abraham was ready to demonstrate his faith by doing the works.

"And Abraham took the wood of the burnt offering, and laid it upon Isaac his son; and he took the fire in his hand, and a knife; and they went both of them together" (Genesis 22:6).

25

Abraham continued to have faith, but he did the works. Line upon line and precept upon precept, Abraham was going to do as commanded by God.

> *"And they came to the place which God had told him of; and Abraham built an altar there, and laid the wood in order, and bound Isaac his son, and laid him on the altar upon the wood. And Abraham stretched forth his hand, and took the knife to slay his son. And the angel of the Lord called unto him out of heaven, and said, Abraham, Abraham: and he said, Here am I. And he said, Lay not thine hand upon the lad, neither do thou any thing unto him: for now I know that thou fearest God, seeing thou hast not withheld thy son, thine only son from me"* (Genesis 22:9-12).

On that altar of faith (and most importantly an altar of works), God swore a blessing upon Abraham that opened his set door for generational blessings.

> *"And said, By myself have I sworn, saith the Lord, for because thou hast done this thing, and hast not withheld thy son, thine only son: That in blessing I will bless thee, and in multiplying I will multiply thy seed as the stars of the heaven, and as the sand which is upon the sea shore; and thy seed shall possess the gate of his enemies; And in thy seed shall all the nations of the earth be blessed; because thou hast obeyed my voice"* (Genesis 22:16-18).

The Abrahamic set door was opened on the platform of "works" for a father of nations, father of faith, friend of God, and hugely successful businessman. Because God saw Abraham's works, He opened to him doors that never existed; doors that had never been opened to any man.

Today, your works will grant you access to generational blessings that eyes have not seen, nor ears heard, in the mighty name of Jesus.

Let Jesus see your works today.

The "Rahabic" Set Door

"Likewise also was not Rahab the harlot justified by works, when she had received the messengers, and had sent them out another way?" (James 2:25)

Another account of works is seen in the story of Rahab, the harlot. Rahab had protected the two spies Joshua sent to Jericho to spy out the land. She had faith and knew their God was a great God, but then she followed up her faith with works by shielding the two spies that Joshua had sent. In Joshua 2:4, we read:

"And the woman took the two men, and hid them, and said thus, There came men unto me, but I wist not whence they were."

We see Rahab expressing her faith in God Almighty, in Joshua 2:9-15:

"And she said unto the men, I know that the Lord hath given you the land, and that your terror is fallen upon us, and that all the inhabitants of the land faint because of you. For we have heard how the Lord dried up the water of the Red sea for you, when ye came out of Egypt; and what ye did unto the two kings of the Amorites, that were on the other side Jordan, Sihon and Og, whom ye utterly destroyed. And as soon as we had heard these things, our hearts did melt, neither did there remain any more courage in any man, because of you: for the Lord

27

your God, he is God in heaven above, and in earth beneath. Now therefore, I pray you, swear unto me by the Lord, since I have shewed you kindness, that ye will also shew kindness unto my father's house, and give me a true token: And that ye will save alive my father, and my mother, and my brethren, and my sisters, and all that they have, and deliver our lives from death. And the men answered her, Our life for yours, if ye utter not this our business. And it shall be, when the Lord hath given us the land, that we will deal kindly and truly with thee. Then she let them down by a cord through the window: for her house was upon the town wall, and she dwelt upon the wall."

Rahab's singular work of faith prepared the way for the Rahabic set door and allowed her name to be included in the lineage of Jesus. There is a set door for you. Only Jehovah sets the door, and only He can open it. I decree that your set door is opened, in Jesus' name.

Kingdom Advancement Factor

"But seek ye first the kingdom of God, and his righteousness; and all these things shall be added unto you" (Matthew 6:33).

The most authentic catalyst of your set door is what I call the **Kingdom advancement factor** or **Kingdom stewardship.** The principle in Matthew 6:33 of "first seeking God's Kingdom and His righteousness" is indeed the basis for becoming a builder of destinies, the maker of kings; and the only valid key to your productive and successful greener pastures on earth.

My early days in dental school were filled with a lack of direction and purpose. As much as I was enjoying studying and aspiring to be the best dentist ever, I felt empty and longed for something more. It was something I could not really describe. In hindsight, all that I was able to achieve then was by the mercy and grace of God, which I certainly did not deserve.

Although, I felt God's love and favor, I didn't really know Him. I was surrounded by friends and roommates who were born-again Christians but I did not know what it meant to be born-again. I was invited to several of their churches and campus fellowships, but would usually fall asleep once the sermons started. I would attend and leave each meeting unchanged. Fortunately, my friends were praying for me. I observed that every time I needed something, even without praying but just by thinking about it, I would get spontaneous answers to my needs out of nowhere. It was not even that I knew to pray about my needs at the time.

One certain day, I remember talking to God and saying, "Wait a minute, why do you answer my prayers so quickly, even when I really don't know you? What will happen when I begin to serve you and go to church?" Immediately, I heard that gentle voice telling me about Matthew 6:33.

He literally said, *"Serve me, make me 'first', and I will bless you and add more to you than you could ever ask for."* He was telling me that I needed to make room for Him first and my set doors would be opened; to seek Him, and watch Him add to me beyond measure. This has stuck with me since that time, and I am a testament to what God can do when you keep your end of the bargain.

For me at that point, the deal that would change my life forever was already ordained, even though I did not quite understand what it involved. In 1996, I surrendered my life completely to Jesus Christ. My friend, Yinka, had invited me to Winners Chapel (Living Faith Church Worldwide), then headquartered in Lagos, Nigeria. It was quite a distance from school, and we did not have a car at the time; so, we had to hop on the popular yellow transit buses called "danfo" to go to church.

Although I did not understand why anyone would want to go through all that trouble for church, for some reason, I followed her. What I experienced while Bishop David Oyedepo was preaching was unforgettable. I gazed at him and wandered, *what manner of preaching is this?* For the first time, I did not sleep during the sermon, and I knew a miracle had taken place in my heart. I wanted more and more of that Word. I began going to church by myself without invitations. I followed hard after God, and I have not looked back since then.

Matthew 6:33 also happens to be the landmark ministry scripture for Bishop David Oyedepo, who is my spiritual father. Getting to know the man behind the ministry, becoming a member of Winners Chapel, and fulfilling the Great Commission was the gift and the lifeline that God blessed me with in 1996.

Bishop Oyedepo is passionate about serving God and His Kingdom with his whole heart. The benefits and blessings that have followed Bishop Oyedepo as a result of his commitment are immeasurable. He has modeled and taught us all how to put the Kingdom of God first in all we do.

Elements of Kingdom Advancement Work

Kingdom advancement work must include prayer for church growth, prayer for lost souls, and prayer for the sick. The grace to do His will, knowing fully well that there is a reward, is the greatest Kingdom secret ever known. It has also become my lifeline.

The Work of Church Growth

In 2014, my business was barely two years old and had been struggling financially, to the point that I could not pay my rent and we were facing eviction. A day before the eviction, I had not packed anything. I left the office intact because I had so much peace that God would do something. I was bent on trusting God for the finances needed even though the situation looked bleak.

When I got home, a light bulb went off in my head. I heard my spiritual father's voice saying, "When you don't know what else to do, praise God, as praise is all He needs us to do." I went on and praised God for about thirty minutes. It was barely three minutes after the praise session ended when my phone rang, and my girlfriend called, promising to bring the funds I needed. God miraculously saved my practice from the mouth of the lion!

This whole experience caused me to ask many questions, the most predominant of which was: *Lord, what do I need to do so that I never find myself in this situation again?* I began to increase my Kingdom advancement factor.

First, in 2015 (tagged the Prophetic Year of Wonder Double), I had the privilege to serve in the core operations team charged with doubling the membership of the church. As I worked tirelessly, I watched God double the number of active patients in my practice. We were averaging new patients at triple the national average per month. As the church grew through my engagement with the works of the Kingdom, my business grew and multiplied. As testimonies rolled into the church, my business, Shalom Dental was also receiving an immense amount of awesome reviews.

I have a friend and dental colleague in Florida with whom I speak all the time. One day, she asked, "What time do you have for the practice? Every time I call, you are either at church or you're on your way there." I smiled and thanked God because He alone took my practice from lack into plenty. Shalom Dental has become a blessing and has never known a better yesterday.

It is a privilege to serve God and work in His vineyard. Since God becomes your employer, can you imagine getting paid by Him? With God, the value of your paycheck is beyond what money can buy; joy and peace in the Holy Ghost are added on and they become your identity as you work for Him.

In every labor, there is profit. Bishop Oyedepo always says, "God is not a user of men." God is indeed not a user of men but a destiny maker and a destiny changer. I trust that as you begin to work in His vineyard, God will decorate your life with His abundant glory, in the mighty name of Jesus.

Secondly, I did the work of tithing the business through the wisdom God gave to me on how to tithe effectively. This was a game-changer, for the blessings of God have since been accruing.

The Work of Winning Souls for Christ

Reconciling men and women back to God was the primary business of Jesus when He started His ministry. When Jesus was a young boy, He accompanied His parents to the temple. Jesus' parents thought they had lost their son and went looking for Him. When they found Him, Jesus said, *"How is it that ye sought me? wist ye not that I must be about my Father's business?"* (Luke 2:49). Clearly, Jesus was telling His parents that His primary job was tending to His Father's business and nothing else mattered.

As redeemed children of God, we automatically inherit the business of our Father, which is to win souls. In the natural world, a father would want his children to take over the business and keep the family legacy. The story of the prodigal son, found in Luke 15:11-32, shows what happens when a child chooses to go his or her own way. No natural father is happy to see their children abandon the family business. The same goes for our heavenly Father. Doing our heavenly Father's business is an important prequalification for accessing your set door of glory and wonder.

Even though there are two types of businesses – the

spiritual business and the physical business – the spiritual business of winning souls should be our primary goal. As we fulfill that purpose, the physical business that God has entrusted into our hands will flourish like the palm tree.

> *"And they that be wise shall shine as the brightness of the firmament; and they that turn many to righteousness as the stars for ever and ever"* (Daniel 12:3).

Going after lost souls and winning souls for the Kingdom of God are guaranteed door openers. Soul winning for Christ touches the heart of God, since souls are His heartbeat. Your stardom is established when you enlist in God's soul-winning army. Since no one has the capability to stop a star from shining, enlisting to win others to Christ enables you to become unstoppable. The enemy cannot bring you down. You will remain on top in your career, business, and ministry. As the stars are above only, so shall your life be.

Be encouraged! You may encounter situations where people may wonder why you do too much. Just stay focused; do not get distracted or discouraged by demonic agents, some of whom are in the church, to derail you from reaching your high calling in Christ and winning the prize which is your set door of greatness.

The Work of Praying Kingdom Advancement Prayers

The mindset of praying for the advancement of the church and doing it first before anything else is a prerequisite for your set door.

Imagine the following. You wake up in the morning and breakfast for Mom while she is still in bed. Then you proceed to the water hose and wash Dad's car. Dad, seeing his shiny car as he gets ready for work, says, "Good job, Son!" If you then decide to ask Dad for money, I believe he will gladly give you whatever you ask because he and Mom are pleased with you. The same goes with God. Praying for the advancement of His Kingdom puts you in a good position to receive His glorious blessings.

The Work of Good Deeds

"What doth it profit, my brethren, though a man say he hath faith, and have not works? can faith save him? If a brother or sister be naked, and destitute of daily food, And one of you say unto them, Depart in peace, be ye warmed and filled; notwithstanding ye give them not those things which are needful to the body; what doth it profit? Even so faith, if it hath not works, is dead, being alone." (James 2:14-17).

The Work of "Thy Neighbor's Keeper"

*"Because I delivered the poor that cried, and the fatherless, and him that had none to help him. The blessing of him that was ready to perish came upon me: and I caused the widow's heart to sing for joy. I put on righteousness, and it clothed me: my judgment was as a robe and a diadem. **I was eyes to the blind, and feet was I to the lame.** I was a father to the poor: and the cause which I knew not I searched out. And I break the jaws of the wicked and plucked the spoil out of his teeth. Then I said, I shall die in my nest, and I shall multiply my days as the sand"* (Job 29:12-18).

35

Job was recorded as a friend of God. God boasted about Job, and Job was also a wealthy businessman. But how did he attain this status? He was eyes to the blind and feet to the lame. He did not pass a blind man by and merely say "God bless you" but made sure to clothe and feed him. This was the secret of how Job became wealthy and loved by God. Job's set door was opened on the basis of his works. When we follow Job's example of caring for those in need, we are practicing the "Job principle".

When God comes looking, will He see your works?

"I know thy works"... (Revelation 2:2).

Are you a billboard or a yard sign for Jesus? Has He seen your works? Jesus not only sees but also records. Do you have a record with God that lists your works? How far are you willing to go in serving God? Are you choosing to be a yard sign or a billboard?

Your works of Kingdom advancement guarantees God's presence. That presence is an automatic door opener. The Red Sea experienced the presence of God when He parted the water. In the same way, the Jordan River experienced the presence of God when it was driven back.

Adam lost the presence of God in the Garden of Eden because of disobedience. He was banished alongside Eve and the doors were shut behind them. To what extent are you experiencing the presence of God?

Jealously guard the presence of God through your works to secure your eternal set door – a door of God's unending and immeasurable blessings that make rich and add no sorrow.

Reflection Questions

What did you learn from the Abrahamic Set Door, the Rahabic Set Door, and the Catalytic Door Openers?

What changes do you need to make in order for the Lord to open those doors?

What works of the Kingdom are you involved in?

CHAPTER FOUR

PREQUALIFIERS FOR YOUR SET DOOR: FAITH

*"I know thy works: behold, I have set before thee an open
door, and no man can shut it: for thou hast a little strength,
and hast kept my word, **and hast not denied my name** "
(Revelation 3:8).*

Your faith and trust in God are a guarantee to open
your set door. Having faith like Abraham, Rahab,
Gideon and others listed in the Hall of Faith in Hebrews
11 will surely throw open your set door.

Like Abraham who was tested concerning Isaac and did
not fail, so will you also be tested. You will be tried in the
fire, in the storm, and in the flood as you enter your set
door, but you will not crumble or be found wanting, in
Jesus' name.

Keeping the word of God is having faith without
staggering, just like Abraham.

*"He staggered not at the promise of God through unbelief;
but was strong in faith, giving glory to God; And being fully
persuaded that, what he had promised, he was able also to*

perform" (Romans 4:20-21).

Faith is a key; it is the language your set door understands in order for it to open. Remember:

> *"...without faith it is impossible to please him: for he that cometh to God must believe that he is, and that he is a rewarder of them that diligently seek him"* (Hebrews 11:6).

How far are you willing to trust God and believe Him in any situation? Are you ready for your set door? Through thick and thin, through the wilderness experience, will you trust God?

Since Jesus set His eyes on the salvation and glory that His death would bring to us, He was willing to be bruised and chastised. He was willing to have the crown of thorns laid on His head. He was willing to be beaten and spat on by men. Even though Jesus was fatigued and fainting, He continued all the way to the cross. He never gave up. In the Garden of Gethsemane, He prayed that the cup might pass over Him, but swiftly added *"...nevertheless not my will, but thine, be done"* (Luke 22:42). Walking in God's will can be the hardest thing to do in many cases, but it is the only pathway to your set door.

> *"...shew me thy faith without thy works, and I will shew thee my faith by my works"* (James 2:18).

Jesus, the author and the finisher of our faith, went all the way to the cross, and He eventually purchased the set door of salvation, riches, glory, power, honor, blessing, and wisdom for us through His blood.

"Saying with a loud voice, Worthy is the Lamb that was slain to receive power, and riches, and wisdom, and strength, and honour, and glory, and blessing" (Revelation 5:12).

God promised to never leave us nor forsake us. The flames will come and so will the storms, but His words are "*Yea and Amen*". Stand in faith, and it will speak for you. Even for the repentant thief on the cross, his set door to heaven opened at the last minute, as he surrendered in faith to the Lordship of Jesus.

I dare you to stand firm on the Rock of Ages, as I believe with you that the set door with your name on it will surely open in the mighty name of Jesus.

Reflection Questions

In what areas of your life is God stretching your faith before He can open your set door?

How far are you willing to trust God and believe Him in any situation?

What has hindered your willingness to trust God through thick and thin and through the wilderness experience?

CHPATER FIVE

THE PASSCODES OF YOUR SET DOOR

"For by him were all things created, that are in heaven, and that are in earth, visible and invisible, whether they be thrones, or dominions, or principalities, or powers: all things were created by him, and for him: And he is before all things, and by him all things consist" (Colossians 1:16-17).

The authenticity of your set door is proven by your ability to access it. Jesus is the door opener. He alone can shut, and He alone can open. No man has the capability to shut what God has not shut. The only true and authentic door - the door of peace, joy and life - is the one the God of heaven and earth has set for you. All things exist in Him.

If it is your set door, it will open for you. It will sense your good works and your faith. It will sense your dependability on God for access, and it will open with ease. You do not have to kick open your set door; it opens for you when your obedience cycle is complete - when you have done not just the good will, but the perfect will of God.

43

Year in and year out, many have been standing at the wrong door. Things have not worked quite well for them, and they are frustrated and discouraged. If this describes you, check the authenticity of your door by being sensitive to the Holy Spirit. The lack of sensitivity to the set door ordained for you by God leads to struggle and frustration. The Holy Spirit is not the author of confusion; He will lead and guide you aright as you are sensitive to His leading. It does not matter how long you stand or knock at a door; it will not open unless you have the correct key or passcode.

The Passcode to Your Set Door is by the Power of the Holy Ghost

"I know thy works: behold, I have set before thee an open door, and no man can shut it: for thou hast a little strength, and hast kept my word, and hast not denied my name" (Revelation 3:8).

Accessing your set door is not by your power nor by your might; it is by the Spirit of God.

"Then he answered and spake unto me, saying, This is the word of the Lord unto Zerubbabel, saying, Not by might, nor by power, but by my spirit, saith the Lord of hosts" (Zechariah 4:6).

Your set door cannot be accessed in the power of your flesh because your strength is completely out of the equation. The children of Israel walked through the wilderness for forty years after they left Egypt, but they were not physically or mentally drained of their strength because they went in the power of God. They had manna from heaven for food; as well as a pillar of cloud by the day and a pillar of fire at night for guidance. This was purely the hand of God leading them all the way, until they got to their set door – the Promised Land.

The Bible says,

> *"He will keep the feet of his saints, and the wicked shall be silent in darkness; for by strength shall no man prevail" (1 Samuel 2:9).*

David, the shepherd boy, took Goliath down, not by any strength of his own, seeing he was just a young shepherd boy; rather, he approached Goliath with a boost of strength from the Holy Ghost.

> *"Then said David to the Philistine, Thou cometh to me with a sword, and with a spear, and with a shield: but I come to thee in the name of the LORD of hosts, the God of the armies of Israel, whom thou hast defied" (1 Samuel 17:45).*

David walked away with Goliath's head and accessed his set door to kingship and the throne. He became a man after God's heart. It is time for you to engage the Holy Ghost like David did. The shepherd boy became the king; David went from the forest to the palace.

I decree, in the name of Jesus, that your set doors will be opened. I decree the word of life upon your tongue right now to speak as the Lord wills. I decree in the name of Jesus, that your set door be opened, in Jesus' name.

The Holy Spirit is our helper and guide. Your sensitivity to His ministry is pivotal to how far you will go in life.

God specializes in using the weak things to confirm His wisdom. God does not need your skills or academic prowess to access your set door; in fact, He wants to use that weakness of yours to show forth His glory.

The enemy may have labeled you barren, and you may be afraid to preach Jesus for fear they will ask, "Where is your God?" But until you go out in your weakness and trust God to use you in your weak state, your set door of fruitfulness may remain shut.

I heard a testimony of a woman with a cancerous mouth, emitting a terrible mouth odor; but she went out daily to preach. No one could even give attention to her words because of the offensive odor. The stench was unbearable. People questioned her and asked her to tell her God to heal her first. Well, as the story was told, God indeed visited her and healed her of cancer.

2 Kings 7:3-8 tells an interesting story:

> *"And there were four leprous men at the entering in of the gate: and they said one to another, why sit we here until we die?*
>
> *If we say, we will enter the city, then the famine is in the city, and we shall die there: and if we sit still here, we die also. Now therefore come and let us fall unto the host of the Syrians: if they save us alive, we shall live; and if they kill us, we shall but die.*
>
> *And they rose up in the twilight, to go unto the camp of the Syrians: and when they were come to the uttermost part of the camp of Syria, behold, there was no man there.*

For the LORD had made the host of the Syrians to hear a noise of chariots, and a noise of horses, even the noise of a great host: and they said one to another, Lo, the king of Israel hath hired against us the kings of the Hittites, and the kings of the Egyptians, to come upon us. Wherefore they arose and fled in the twilight, and left their tents, and their horses, and their asses, even the camp as it was, and fled for their life.

And when these lepers came to the uttermost part of the camp, they went into one tent, and did eat and drink, and carried thence silver, and gold, and raiment, and went and hid it; and came again, and entered into another tent, and carried thence also, and went and hid it."

The four lepers in their weakness arose in courage against all odds and went forward; as a result, they lived. God took over, and the set door of their new lives was opened. Not only was theirs opened but their courage opened up the door of life to their nation.

I pray that this day God will grant you the courage to rise and enter your set door with your name on it, in Jesus' name. Come as you are and trust that the Holy Spirit will do a work in you, setting you on high for your set door which ultimately leads to many more doors.

The Word

The word of God is life, giving you strength as you consume it. The word of God is the backbone of your faith. The word of God fuels your faith to generate the power needed to carry out the works. The word of God is the hammer breaking every obstacle on your way. The word of God is a mirror image that reflects who you can be and what your set door looks like. The word of God is true and all-powerful. Engaging the word of God through prayers and supplication is the secret weapon that the enemy never wants you to take advantage of. It strips away the layers of all barriers on your path and allows access to the treasures behind your set door. Line by line and precept by precept, the word of God takes off layers and veils that the enemy uses to derail us.

The Blood of Jesus

"And they overcame him by the blood of the Lamb, and by the word of their testimony; and they loved not their lives unto the death" (Revelation 12:11).

The blood of Jesus, the sacrificial Lamb of God, is the unstoppable weapon of God at our disposal for a total knock-out of the enemy in the battle arena. We see a precursor to the redemptive power in the blood in Exodus 12 when God instructed the Israelites through Moses to place the blood of a lamb on the side and upper door posts of their homes. This was God's last card for the release of the children of Israel after their 430 years of bondage in Egypt.

Prior to the blood of the lamb being spread on the side and upper door posts of their homes, God had deployed nine plagues in Egypt in order to change Pharaoh's mind to let His people go. Pharaoh remained adamant and would not let the Israelites go and worship their God. When God was set to execute final judgment on Pharaoh and his cohorts, He commanded the blood to be applied on the door posts of the Israelites' households in order to separate them from those of the Egyptians. That same night, God completely turned the heart of Pharaoh by slaying his first born.

"And it came to pass, that at midnight the LORD smote all the firstborn in the land of Egypt, from the firstborn of Pharaoh that sat on his throne unto the firstborn of the captive that was in the dungeon; and all the firstborn of cattle" (Exodus 12:29).

There was great wailing and mourning in the land, for it was not until the last card – the blood of the first born lamb – was applied that Pharaoh urgently called for Moses and literally begged him to take his people and leave Egypt immediately.

"And he called for Moses and Aaron by night, and said, Rise up, and get you forth from among my people, both ye and the children of Israel; and go, serve the LORD, as ye have said.

Also take your flocks and your herds, as ye have said, and be gone; and bless me also.

And the Egyptians were urgent upon the people, that they might send them out of the land in haste; for they said, we be all dead men" (Exodus 12: 31-33).

The aftermath of engaging this last weapon was the liberation of the Israelites. Their set door of freedom, peace, and joy was flung open by the power of the blood of the lamb.

I decree, in Jesus' name, that your set door be opened this day by the blood of Jesus, the blood of the everlasting covenant, the blood that speaks better things than the blood of Abel's sacrifice.

Alignment and Right Positioning with God

There is a defined order in the Kingdom of God. Things can only work for us if we are properly aligned to the door opener, Jesus. Where you stand and who you stand with determine what flows to you.

> *"Behold, how good and how pleasant it is for brethren to dwell together in unity!*
>
> *It is like the precious ointment upon the head, that ran down upon the beard, even Aaron's beard: that went down to the skirts of his garments.*
>
> *As the dew of Hermon, and as the dew that descended upon the mountains of Zion: for there the* LORD *commanded the blessing, even life for evermore"* (Psalm 133: 1-3).

The blessing flows from the head to the feet. Are you in proper alignment with God and the spiritual authority God has placed over you? You cannot say someone is your spiritual father and yet do not obey any instructions in their church. If you are just there to create chaos, then you are out of alignment.

> *"And we beseech you, brethren, to know them which labor among you, and are over you in the Lord, and admonish you; And to esteem them very highly in love for their work's sake. And be at peace among yourselves"* (1 Thessalonians 5:12-13).

God used the example of birds flying together in unison

to show the truth of this verse in my life. One day, as I saw my husband to the door on his way to work, the Holy Spirit asked me to look up, and I as did I saw a flock of birds flying together synchronously; it was a beautiful sight to behold. Then the Holy Spirit ministered to me and said, "Do you see how beautiful they appear when they fly together in such harmony? Compare it to when they fly in different directions and not in sync – the chaos makes it difficult for you to appreciate their beauty." Then He declared, "Nike, be in alignment. Be aligned with your spiritual fathers; it beautifies you and crowns you with grace and honor. Every gift they carry flows from their head to you, if you are properly aligned and in position."

It is impossible to be out of alignment with God and the spiritual fathers that He has placed over you and still enjoy the blessings of God. If you are running a race and go off the track, you will be disqualified and not be in any position to win. But remember, this shall not be your portion, in Jesus' name. Staying in alignment and position is a recipe for your set door of greatness to be opened; this will enable you to live a life free of frustration and failure, in Jesus' name. Ask yourself the alignment question: Am I on-track or off-track?

You cannot claim the promises of God and disregard His principles. Get back on track with your maker and those whom He has put over you; His promises for your life shall be fulfilled, in Jesus' name. Your set door is undeniable when you are in alignment.

Reflection Questions

Since your set door cannot be accessed in the power of your flesh because your strength is completely out of the equation, what changes is the Holy Spirit nudging you to make in your life?

What is needed for you to stay in alignment and rightly positioned so that you can claim the promises of God for your life?

CHAPTER SIX

SENSITIVITY TO TIMES AND SEASONS

"To everything there is a season, and a time to every purpose under the heaven..." (Ecclesiastes 3:1-8).

Our God is a God of timing. Times and seasons are critical to the Lord in running divine programs and opening set doors. An understanding of God's timeline puts you right in the center of His agenda.

"For the vision is yet for an appointed time, but at the end it shall speak, and not lie: though it tarry, wait for it; because it will surely come, it will not tarry" (Habakkuk 2:3).

God is always speaking, but we are not always listening, let alone following His instructions. There is always what to do per time as seasons come and go. You cannot call forth cold weather in the summer and vice versa.

Every true set door for your life has a divinely appointed time, and you must be sensitive to receive it. Your appointed time is now, in Jesus' name!

"And of the children of Issachar, which were men that understood the times, to know what Israel ought to do; the heads of them were two hundred; and all their brethren were at their commandment" (1 Chronicles 12:32).

Developing spiritual sensitivity is critical to stimulating spiritual alertness. Men that have been known to attain great heights in accessing their set doors in Christ were men of supernatural sensitivity to the Holy Spirit.

The voice of the Spirit is a supernatural door opener. Isaiah 48:17 says,

> *"Thus saith the Lord, thy Redeemer, the Holy one of Israel: I am the Lord thy God, who teacheth thee to profit who leadeth thee by the way that thou shouldest go."*

The ability to hear the voice of God in order to know what to do in season is an asset. Until you hear God, no one will hear you. Until you enter your set door, no one will hear you.

Prayer

> *May you not miss your time of visitation, in the mighty name of Jesus.*

Reflection Questions

What have been some specific instances when you have heard the voice of God?

What is God speaking to your heart as you read this book so that you can have your set door opened?

Chapter Seven
Catalytic Door Openers

Mentorship

Accessing your set door is also by prophetic utterance. God has put people on your path to activate your set door.

> *"Thus saith the LORD, stand ye in the ways, and see, and ask for the old paths, where is the good way, and walk therein, and ye shall find rest for your souls. But they said, we will not walk therein"* (Jeremiah 6:16).

> *"That ye be not slothful, but followers of them who through faith and patience inherit the promises"* (Hebrews 6:12).

There is a place for mentorship in accessing your set door. What you need for your next phase is in the hands of someone God has placed over you. You can only access this key through meekness, humility, and a thirst for what they have that will help you on your journey. The mentors who God places in your life carry unction, wisdom, and grace that need to be imparted to you. Find your mentors and access that which God has put in their hands for your set door of breakthrough to be opened.

Sacrifice

This is probably the handiest catalyst required to open your set door, but many don't take advantage of it. Perhaps because they lack grace for giving. Maybe they lack grace to lay down a sacrifice like Abraham did with Isaac, or they simply lack knowledge about the enormous power of sacrifice. Just as we saw earlier, obedience which led to sacrifice was the singular act by Abraham that caused God to place a generational blessing on him.

> *"And Abraham stretched forth his hand and took the knife to slay his son.*
>
> *And the angel of the* LORD *called unto him out of heaven, and said, Abraham, Abraham: and he said, here am I.*
>
> *And he said, lay not thine hand upon the lad, neither do thou anything unto him: for now, I know that thou fearest God, seeing thou hast not withheld thy son, thine only son from me"* (Genesis 22:10-12).

My very first encounter with the power of sacrifice was in 1999 at the Winner's Chapel yearly conference called "Shiloh" when the ark of sacrifice was enacted. My bishop had called for a sacrifice, and everyone was to sacrifice according to what God had laid on their hearts. I had never done one before, but I heard expressly from God to give my salary from the previous month and my air conditioner in the room where I was living during my residency at the Lagos University Teaching Hospital. It was the most expensive asset that I had and every attempt from my end to negotiate the deal with God was not fruitful. I had dropped my last paycheck, but He was still asking for my air conditioning unit, which I had planned to take to my family home since we did not have one at that time. For my single mother, who struggled to provide food for us, that air conditioner would have been a luxury.

After some time of struggling and hoping God would forget, I obeyed God's prompting to sacrifice by finally calling a friend who had a car. My friend and I dropped off the air conditioning unit at the church premises.

After this, my set door opened automatically, with every request granted, way beyond my wildest dreams. It was a catalytic downpour of blessings. Every single item on my prayer request list was answered, including one I did not make – my living in America today.

I got my dream job at that time, working at the Office of the Presidency, which at the time was the only position of its kind. I got my dream car in the exact color I had seen in my dreams, and I did not have to pay a dime. I called it my angelic car. Not only that, I started making double my previous salary, and I got married to the man of my dreams. The sacrifice I made then was indeed a catalytic door opener!

If you can lay it down, you will surely pick it up again beyond measure, as God is faithful to fulfill His word. The sacrifice at the altar has opened many more doors for me and my family. After trying for six years without having children, I had a conversation with God. I said no to *in vitro* fertilization since it was not guaranteed; instead, I sacrificed the money I would have used for it. After that, we had our first child and then a second. Even when we said, "Lord, we are good," a third (and the last child) as promised by God came into our household.

The altar of sacrifice is the altar of turn-around testimonies. It is an amazing door opener. It is a supernatural catalyst that sets up a chain of unbelievable miraculous acts of God in your life.

Prayer

I pray for you this day that the grace to lay down a sacrifice at the right time and season will lead to your set door of glory and locate you today.

Reflection Questions

Who has God placed in your life to mentor you so that you can have your set door opened?

What sacrificial gifts is the Lord asking you to make so that He can continue to lead you to your set door?

Chapter Eight

The Door Busters

There are door busters with the capability to create a force entry to your set door.

Prayer and Fasting

There is without a doubt a set door of uncommon riches and glory set for us, but we cannot gain entrance cheaply without fighting the good fight of faith.

> *"This charge I commit unto thee, son Timothy, according to the prophecies which went before on thee, that thou by them mightiest war a good warfare"* *(1 Timothy 1:18-19).*

> *"For a great door and effectual is opened unto me, and there are many adversaries (1 Corinthians 16:9).*

There is a contention for your set door. Fight the good fight of faith with prayer and fasting. Fasting is a door buster.

After graduating as a Doctor of Dental Surgery, I knew I only wanted to work briefly for an employer before starting my practice. Even though I was working a few days a week, I spent the rest of the time going from pillar to post, looking for opportunities for my own place.

Every attempt to obtain the startup finances fell short.

I was very concerned but had faith that God would do it. I attended a July power explosion at a church in Maryland where Pastor Matthew Ashimolowo ministered and encouraged us to sow a seed of completion – $560 - which I joyfully sowed, trusting God to perfect my career and give me my own place.

At the end of the service, as the Holy Spirit urged me to sow into the life of the pastor, I began complaining bitterly to God about how I had sown all the money I made that week at my part-time job and barely had anything left (which is laughable, now that I think about it). But I obeyed, and I scrambled to write a second check to the tune of $100. "Now what?" I asked God. "How do I find the pastor in this crowd?"

I stood in front of the church pondering on this with the check in my hand, ready to go. Then I heard some scrambling behind me. As I looked back, I saw the pastor, surrounded by his pastoral aides, coming toward me. I, however, was able to press in and handed him the check. I also asked him to pray for me, as I explained my plight and the struggle to find financing to get my practice started. He gave me specific instructions to fast for five Fridays and read Psalms 27 at least three times a day. So, I started the fast immediately.

Just before that encounter, I had a dream. In that dream, my husband and I were in the car and the whole place was flooded, with no way out. There were other cars trapped in addition to ours, and it seemed like we were going around in circles. Suddenly a man showed up jogging in shorts and his athletics jacket. I was not sure how he was able to jog since water was everywhere. I beckoned him and asked him to please show us the way out and he pointed to a street sign with "Oak Grove Rd" on it. When I woke up, I began wondering what the dream meant. I understood we had been tossed back and forth by the banks due to insufficient credit, but I felt strongly that God had shown the way out. We just did not know how to find that way.

Coincidentally, my encounter with the pastor was shortly after having the dream. On the first Friday of the fast, the Holy Spirit brought to my remembrance the dream and the sign. As I continued to ponder on the pieces of the revelation, I wondered if "Oaks Grove" was the name of a financial institution. I searched online and behold there was a bank with that name. I called the bank on the Monday following the first of my five-week Friday-only fasts. Although the bank representative said that they did not do start-up financing, he referred me to a bank that did. I called the recommended bank, got an automated voicemail, and left a message.

The next day I got a call back, and the bank was willing to begin the financing process, even though the hour-long interrogation with the banker seemed strange. All of this occurred with a crying baby on one hand and trying to answer the questions correctly; it seemed like he was just trying to convince himself about my loan worthiness. After the unending interrogation, he finally said, "There is no reason for us to deny you this loan."

By the second Friday of my fast – two days after the long interrogation – the heavens opened. I received a call stating that I had been granted the loan to start up the dental practice. Lo and behold, on August 15, 2011, the Monday after the third Friday of my fast, the approval for Shalom Dental was announced. An unbelievable miracle of a lifetime was finally birthed, after years of trying unsuccessfully. What an awesome God we serve!

It has been eight years since Shalom Dental opened its doors, and it has continuously been His business where we have been blessing lives and restoring hope to every patient that walks into the practice. God is truly a God that decrees, and it comes to pass. He causes water to come out of the rock; He makes a way where there is no way – a God of miracles, signs, and wonders, who has never left Himself without a witness. God is so real and faithful; we must be sensitive to His voice and trust Him to guide us to our set door.

After that whole encounter, a light bulb went up in my head as to why Friday was the chosen fast day. I realized no one really liked fasting on Fridays, being the beginning of the weekend. Fridays were fun day due to ceremonies and parties with so much food to tempt one. Who could then imagine the thought of fasting on such a day, - which is why I think it was so potent for me! That is not to say fasting on other days of the week is not powerful. Any day that you decide to engage your heart in fasting, heaven will answer.

Although, I still fast on other days, I believe there is a

supernatural grace and power that makes fasting on a Friday a super effective way to open your set door. Any day you choose to engage your heart, however, is the day your door opens. I shared my unique experience with fasting on Fridays because I think that day should be utilized more since it comes with a unique sacrifice.

Fasting is a door buster. Fast with your heart and with a sense of purpose, accompanied with dying to your flesh – the god of your belly – so that the glory of the Lord can rise upon you. Fasting is a sacrifice that must be paid in order for you to have anything of Kingdom value handed to you. Having my own practice opened me up to another world - one of open doors and even more open doors. God is faithful.

Remember you are hidden in Christ Jesus. Through your redemption in Christ, you are born victorious. It is time to wage war against every barrier to your set door. Stop watching it close on you; kick it open by engaging the power of the Holy Spirit through prayer and fasting.

Praying in the Spirit

The Holy Ghost is your guide to your set door; therefore, engage with Him in the spirit through prayer. Spirit-led prayers will catapult you to your set door and have the devil running out of breath trying to chase you. You will be too far gone for the enemy to catch up with you.

The Holy Ghost will imbue you with power to dismantle every satanic installation against your access to your set door.

"And behold, I send the promise of my Father upon you: but tarry ye in the city of Jerusalem, until ye be endued with power from on high" (Luke 24:49).

The Holy Ghost will grant you access to the deep things of God so you know what to do and how to get through your set door.

"Howbeit, when he, the Spirit of truth, is come, he will guide you into all truth; for he shall not speak of himself; but whatsoever he shall hear, that shall he speak; and he will shew you things to come" (John 16:13).

The Holy Ghost will fuel your prayer life so you can press, until you gain access.

"Likewise, the Spirit also helped our infirmities: for we know not what we should pray for as we ought: but the Spirit itself makes intercession for us with groanings which cannot be uttered. And he that searched the hearts knoweth what is the mind of the Spirit, because he makes intercession for the saints according to the will of God" (Romans 8: 26-27).

Thanksgiving

"And at midnight Paul and Silas prayed, and sang praises unto God; and the prisoners heard them. And suddenly there was a great earthquake, so that the foundations of the prison were shaken: and immediately all the doors were opened, and every one's bands were loosed. And the keeper of the prison awaking out of his sleep, and seeing the prison doors open, he drew out his sword, and would have killed himself, supposing that the prisoners had been fled" (Acts 16:25-27).

Paul and Silas first prayed, and then they praised: Hallelujah, the prison doors were thrown open. They were liberated into their God ordained set door. When you praise, there is a shaking in the heavenlies. The signal transmitted to heaven when you praise God is undeniable. It halts heaven and gets heavenly attention. Praise is an undeniable door opener.

The Psalmist in Psalm 92:1 says it is a good thing to give thanks to the Lord always (not sometimes). Thanksgiving is a potent force for leveling change. It is an unbeatable signal that transcends heavenly protocols, rising to the throne room of God with an aroma so strong that it can't be missed. The Bible says God inhabits our praise. God lives and breathes praise. When you praise God, you occupy a space near and dear to Him. Praise gets you on the VIP-list where you receive God's attention. No wonder Jesus, in John 11: 41-43, stood at the tomb of Lazarus who had been dead for four days and lifted His hands and said, "Father, thank you." Then He called Lazarus forth from the grave, and Lazarus responded immediately. The dead situation was turned around to a living one, showing the unbelievable demonstration of the power of thanksgiving, even in death. This miracle caused many to believe and opened the set door of validation of Jesus' ministry and the salvation of souls.

As I have shared previously, I had a unique encounter that revolved around the power of thanksgiving. In 2014, barely two years after opening our doors, Shalom Dental was going to be shut down, as I was not able to pay my rent. All the stories I had heard and read about new businesses going under after less than year came to mind. My landlord had already set an eviction date, but I kept trusting God for the money to pay him as I did not want to borrow or take any loan. A day before the eviction, I left the office without packing up anything as I should have done in anticipation of eviction the next day. I got home and met gloomy faces all around; my husband and my mother did not know what else to do at this point. Then inspiration came from heaven. The Holy Spirit brought to my remembrance what my spiritual father Bishop David Oyedepo always said, "When you do not know what else to do, praise Him."

I went downstairs to the basement of my house and praised God for from the depth of my heart for about 30 minutes, then returned upstairs to the rest of the family. I was there, barely 2 minutes when my phone rang; it was a friend whom I had not spoken to in years. She had just called out of the blues wanted to know how I was and what was going on with me. I mentioned the eviction situation, and she said she was going to come the next day with the money I needed to pay the landlord. And that, my friends, was how God saved Shalom Dental from eviction and failure through the power of thanksgiving.

Shalom Dental is now eight years old strong and here to stay. God has made it such that the rent is now something I never have to worry about. God has provided in such a way that the rent gets paid when due without any notices. The set door of financial breakthrough has since opened. The enemy knew that opening this particular set door would not only bless my family, but would also expand the

Kingdom of God. The enemy attempted to shut down Shalom Dental, but God said no! Shalom Dental today, to the glory of God, is a blessing to its world. Praise the Lord!

Thanksgiving is also a multiplier. Lifting the so-called little in your hands and saying, "Father, thank you," does not fail to bring about immeasurable multiplication. We must learn to say thank you, so that we can walk into our set doors. The Israelites did not get into their promised land because they fell prey to murmuring and complaining, leading to many dying in the wilderness. You cannot access your set door through ingratitude. You must remain grateful and thankful at all times.

"...Worthy is the Lamb that was slain to receive power, and riches, and wisdom, and strength, and honor, and glory, and blessing" (Revelation 5:12).

Treasures Behind Your Door – The Peace of God

"And the peace of God, which passeth all understanding, shall keep your hearts and mind through Christ Jesus" (Philippians 4:7).

The treasures behind your set door are immeasurable and unquantifiable and lead to the peace of God that surpasses all understanding and only He can give. The peace of God is something no one can really give you, except God.

In 2017, our church had a major change in leadership, and the hearts of my family were torn on whether to stay or to leave. We had peace for a while daily, trying to justify our decisions at that time. We also prayed earnestly to God to heal our hurt and pain, so we could be where He wanted us to be.

In August 2017, we were on a family vacation and the Lord expanded the understanding of my eyes regarding the Garden of Eden. He expressed to me that as beautiful as He had created the garden for Adam and Eve, the enemy still crept in and corrupted Eve, just to displace man out of his appointed place. This led to man losing favor in His sight and being cast out of the beautiful garden that He had made for them.

As God continued to give me insight, He likened this experience to the church and explained that He has an appointed place for all His children to worship. Since the enemy does not want God's people to partake of the blessings therein, he will seek for ways to displace them. Therefore, he will creep in and sow seeds of anger, wickedness, hatred, and bitterness that can ultimately lead to the division of the church. The Lord mentioned that the enemy will seek to displace His people out of their appointed place of worship from time to time because he knows they will continue to prosper and blossom if left alone in it.

Just as the Garden of Eden was not inaccessible to the devil, he will, therefore, seek to test you in your appointed place. Even though your appointed place is a place of beauty and perfection, it could also be a place of temptation. God, however, will always cause you to come out victorious.

Shortly after that encounter, the peace that was restored to us was unimaginable. Never again have we lost our peace concerning our appointed place of worship. God went on to say that where He had planted me and my family was good and perfect. We must, however, remain on guard because the enemy seeks to displace us daily. We must not give room to the devil.

Even when you are out of alignment with God, if you cry to Him daily to guide you, He steps in and repositions you for peace beyond understanding. The day my family conformed to His plan and returned to our designated place of perfection for worship, our peace was restored. There was a clear difference between my encounter with God before and after my vacation. All unrest vanished once we repositioned and realigned ourselves with God by His power. This "season" was the entry point to our set door of continuous fellowship with God.

Having the peace of God, like my family personally experienced in 2018, is a treasure that only God gives, and it can only be received when you walk through your set door.

Prayer

I decree that your appointed set door be opened to you this day, in Jesus' name. I decree an end to every fruitless journey. May a life of favor, power, glory, honor, and the peace of God that surpasses all understanding be yours, in the mighty name of Jesus.

Reflection Questions

What steps do you need to take to prepare yourself for fasting and praying?

How is the Lord leading you to pray in the Spirit?

For what things do you need to give thanks back to God?

CHAPTER NINE

A WONDER IN YOUR WILDERNESS

I do not know where you are in your relationship with God, but there is an appointed door for your liberty. It may appear dry and hopeless, but God is not done with you. There is a time and a season for everything.

"To everything there is a season, and a time to every purpose under the heaven" (Ecclesiastes 3:1).

The Lord came so you could have life and have it more abundantly (John 10:10). But there is always the question of what to do when you feel that you are going around in circles. There is always a key needed to open the next door, and it always comes down to the keys of Kingdom service and covenant responsibility. We cannot plead God's promises, while breaking His covenant. There is always a Kingdom strategy to unlock your set door.

Six years into our marriage, we were yet to have children. We went from doctor to doctor, and I was eventually diagnosed with cystic ovarian fibrosis. But we kept trusting God daily for our miracle child. Service to the Kingdom of God kept us going. My husband and I were not only committed, but also actively involved in serving God with everything we had, both day and night. One fateful winter morning while driving to school at the University of Maryland Baltimore College of Dental Surgery, the Holy Spirit brought to my attention the gigantic trees lining the sides of the road. He said to me, "Look at these trees; they look dead and lifeless, dry and bare of leaves, and you wonder if they would ever be green again?"

Then he answered the question Himself and said, "Yes, they will." He said that, before the foundation of the earth, He had inputted a survival mechanism into the trees to enable them to survive, even during the dry winter season. The xylem in the stem of trees is a means of storage of water so the trees can feed on that in winter. The same goes for the cactus plants in the desert that have special mechanisms that aid them in storing and conserving water. They bear no leaves, and this helps them to reduce transpiration (loss of water to the atmosphere through leaves).

Your situation may seem hopeless as mine was many years ago but know that there is power on your inside. God is a good Father who has well laid-out plans for good and not evil for everyone that calls upon His name. There is always a set time for everything under the earth. Summer is not forever, and neither is winter. No one season can prevent the other from beginning its cycle. So, while you are in your dry season, there is always something to do.

"For there is hope of a tree, if it be cut down, that it will sprout again, and that the tender branch thereof will not cease. Though

the root thereof wax old in the earth, and the stock thereof die in the ground; Yet through the scent of water it will bud and bring forth boughs like a plant" (Job 14:7-9).

You have not been called to seek God in vain. This too shall pass, so hold your head up. Rev up the engine of your life and serve God. He is our eternal helper.

In the wilderness, God has a set door for you.

"I will lift mine eyes unto the hills, from whence cometh my help. My help cometh from the LORD, which made heaven and earth" (Psalm 121:1-2).

God has a plan for you. There is a set door for you. Now is your appointed time, in Jesus' name. Your season is about to change.

"And ye shall serve the LORD your God, and he shall bless thy bread, and thy water; and I will take sickness away from the midst of thee" (Exodus 23:25).

While I was waiting and serving, God reminded of His word in Psalm 127:3:

"Lo, children are an heritage of the Lord, and the fruit of the womb is his reward."

Children come as a reward of service to God.

When you commit to serving the Lord, sickness departs from your dwelling. Everything is anchored on faithful service; don't be a visitor in your Father's house.

Serving God opens your set door. I pray that God will give you the grace and the empowerment to serve Him joyfully with all your heart, so that you can walk through your set door, in Jesus' name.

I stand in the shoes of my father, Bishop David Oyedepo, and I decree by the blood of Jesus that your set door be opened, in the mighty name of Jesus. Your time is now! Doors open not by power nor by might but by the Spirit of God. The doors of progress, new businesses, children, finances, blessings, honor, glory riches and power be opened to you this day, in Jesus' name.

Today, we have three amazing children. We named the first one *Ayomide*, meaning, "My Joy Has Come." While we were still recovering from the first miracle, the second child showed up without praying. We named her *Iyanuoluwa*, meaning, "Miracle of God". After Iyanuoluwa's birth, we said, "Okay, Lord, we are fully satisfied." I told God I did not want any more children, so I could manage the practice that was just taking off.

How could I say no to having another child, after I had prayed so hard for children for six years? I could not believe I was doing that. But God, having a great sense of humor, said, "Not so fast." I found out I was pregnant again, right as the plans for the practice were finally taking off. I said, "Lord, seriously? I thought we had this conversation? I am okay with two kids!"

The Lord replied calmly, like He always does, and said, "Yes, my daughter, we did; but remember, my blessings make rich and add no sorrow." That settled it for me because I knew He was going to make it all work out for my good, and He certainly did. The last baby came a month before the grand opening of Shalom Dental. I had so much help and favor surrounding me all around. My divinely appointed helpers would not allow me to lift a finger nor do anything after I brought the baby home. We named him *Oluwatobi*, meaning, "God is Great".

My set door of fruitfulness in marriage opened through service to God, even in the midst of my wilderness and dry season. Because of the grace to focus on God, I was able to do what was required of me in that season, serving God. Even though I asked God for triplets to make up for the years I had waited, they came one after the other. After seeing what parenting entailed and saying two children were good, God said, "There would be one more; you asked for it." Bless the name of Jesus!

You are next in line, in Jesus' name.

Reflection Questions

What promises of God from His word can you hold on to during your dry seasons?

You may feel that you are in a hopeless situation, how will you trust God even though you are not be able to see Him working all things out for your good?

CHAPTER TEN

EMBRACE YOUR SET DOOR NOW

There is no doubt that God loves His children, and He longs every day to guide us, if we submit to Him. There is always some direction we can choose to go, but without His guidance we will be lost. This singular passcode is very essential to the fulfillment of our life's purpose.

"For the LORD's portion is his people; Jacob is the lot of his inheritance. He found him in a desert land, and in the waste howling wilderness; he led him about, he instructed him, he kept him as the apple of his eye. As an eagle stirred up her nest, fluttered over her young, spreadeth abroad her wings, taketh them, beareth them on her wings: So the LORD alone did lead him, and there was no strange god with him. He made him ride on the high places of the earth, that he might eat the increase of the fields; and he made him to suck honey out of the rock, and oil out of the flinty rock" (Deuteronomy 32:9-13).

Jacob was meek enough to be guided, and God took him up in His wings and caused him to soar high above all challenges. He alone did lead Jacob, instructing him, encircling him, and enabling him suck oil out of the flinty rock.

"Then I proclaimed a fast there, at the river of Ahava, that we might afflict ourselves before our God, to seek of him a right way for us, and for our little ones, and for all our substance. For I was ashamed to require of the king a band of soldiers and horsemen to help us against the enemy in the way: because we had spoken unto the king, saying, The hand of our God is upon all them for good that seek him; but his power and his wrath is against all them that forsake him. So we fasted and besought our God for this: and he was intreated of us" (Ezra 8:21-23).

When you seek God through prayer and fasting, He will be found by you.

Removing Enemies of Your Set Door - Fear

"For God hath not given us the spirit of fear; but of power, and of love, and of a sound mind" (2 Timothy 1:7).

Do not allow the devices of the enemy to keep you down. Fear is a cheap weapon of the enemy to deny us our set door in Christ. You must replace every spirit of fear with faith. You must create the image of the future you desire and not let the enemy tell you what you can do. The enemy has no hold over you as you are the righteousness of God in Christ Jesus; you are the apple of His eyes.

You are seated in heavenly places in Christ Jesus. You are born to win. Therefore, this day every spirit of fear that has held you back is crushed, in the name of Jesus.

You will never lose a battle again. Your time is now. Lift your head up and walk into your set door of glory and abundance, in Jesus' name

Lastly, if you will take the chance, surrender to Jesus, and love His Kingdom, serving Him in truth, holiness and joy, then you are next in line to access the set door with your name on it through the power of the Holy Ghost.

Your Set Door is Open, Walk through It!

Yes, your set door is opened in the name of Jesus Christ. Not by might, nor by power, but by the Spirit of God. Arise from that pit of reproach and shame, depression and fear, in the name of Jesus, and walk through your preordained door of glory, power, honor, riches, wisdom, and blessings in the name of Jesus.

This is your time, and your long-awaited triumphant entry is now. I dare you to lift up your hands to the Father and see if He will not receive you. He will take you into His mighty and able hands so that you can walk in together. Do not hold back, you are born a victor, not a leper.

You are now the child of the Lord of Lords and the King of Kings. You have access. Congratulations! I cannot wait to hear your testimony in Jesus' mighty name. Amen!

Prayer

Thank you, Lord! Bless me, in Jesus name. I _____ [put your name in] access my set door this day and forever more, in Jesus' name!

Glory to God in the Highest!!

The Set Door Covenant

LORD, I covenant on this day _____ of the month of _____ in the year _____ to seek you first with all of my heart above everything else.

Reflection Questions

Have you given your life to the Lord for salvation?

What will need to change for you to allow the Lord to guide you along the pathway of your set door?

Are you willing to take the chance, surrender to Jesus, love His Kingdom, and serve Him in truth, holiness, and joy so that you can access your set door?

NOTES

_____

_____

_____

_____

_____

_____

_____

_____

_____

_____

_____

_____

_____

_____

NOTES

NOTES

_____

_____

_____

_____

_____

_____

_____

_____

_____

_____

_____

_____

_____

NOTES

_____

_____

_____

_____

_____

_____

_____

_____

_____

_____

_____

_____

NOTES

_____

_____

_____

_____

_____

_____

_____

_____

_____

_____

_____

_____

_____

NOTES

NOTES

_____

_____

_____

_____

_____

_____

_____

_____

_____

_____

_____

_____

_____

NOTES

_____

_____

_____

_____

_____

_____

_____

_____

_____

_____

_____

_____

_____

NOTES

_____

_____

_____

_____

_____

_____

_____

_____

_____

_____

_____

_____

NOTES

NOTES

_____

_____

_____

_____

_____

_____

_____

_____

_____

_____

_____

_____

_____

NOTES

_____

_____

_____

_____

_____

_____

_____

_____

_____

_____

_____

_____

_____

NOTES

_____

_____

_____

_____

_____

_____

_____

_____

_____

_____

_____

_____

_____

Made in the USA
Columbia, SC
22 December 2021

52576493R00057